Everything Leads To Nothing

Endless Roads

Adara Creasman

Made with ❤ on the BookLeaf Publishing Platform

www.bookleafpub.in

www.bookleafpub.com

Dedication

To myself for never giving up & to the ones who helped
me survive you know who you are.

Preface

Small
What lye's beyond
Something I do not know
To be begged would be something
White lips pressed firmly together
Death could cure
Everything
And nothing at all

Acknowledgements

I would like to take a moment to honor and express my deepest gratitude to three souls who have shaped my journey with their love, resilience, and unwavering presence.

To my child self, I see you. I honor your strength, your courage, and the light you never let fade despite the darkness you endured. You survived, you kept going, and because of you, I stand here today. Thank you for your resilience, your hope, and your belief in a future you couldn't yet see. This is for you.

To my loving fiancé, your unwavering support, love, and kindness have been my refuge. Thank you for standing beside me, for believing in me even when I doubted myself, and for reminding me that I am worthy of love and happiness. Your presence in my life is a gift, and I am endlessly grateful for you.

To my grandmother, your wisdom, love, and strength have been my guiding light. You have shown me what it means to endure, to love unconditionally, and to carry the past with grace while still embracing the future. Your lessons and love are woven into everything I do, and I cherish you beyond words.

With all my heart, I thank you.

1. Stained Glass

Stained glass, portraits of lying laughter
I would give anything
To know what your after
Don't pull me on this chain behind you
Please, Just let me walk beside you
I promise I won't speak if you don't want me to
I can be quite
just let me walk beside you.
you'll never know I'm there unless I want you to
Isn't that what I'm Supposed to do?
What more can you ask of me?
I'll give you anything.
Stained glass portraits of hopeless laughter
I would give anything
To know what your after
This chain around my neck is pulling faster
Is suffocation the answer?
what more can you ask of me?
I've given you everything.

Stained glass portraits of broken laughter
I would give anything
To know what your after
Falling doesn't seam so bad
when your six feet under
what more can you ask of me?
This is everything
you have all of me

2. My Confined Mind

Inside my Confined mind
The bars on the windows are unsympathetic to my cause
The ice that covers the walls is dripping all over the floor
What a mess
The floor is wet and covered in gray and black slush
What a mess
The wind whistles through the window glacial and
disappointed
It is dark and murky here
It is cold and lonely here
Inside my confined mind
I sit in silence
Frozen like a statue
Never moving
Peering out into the world I have made for myself
I feel distant and lost
Everything that I have done surrounds me
Inside my confined mind is the only place I feel safe

3. Red Sun

As the red sun sets in the sky
I contemplate , contemplate and I cry
Whole soul sadness
Complete and total loss
Conscious decision to just ...not
The water bubbles and flows
In endless circles it goes
Shattered minds
Twisted
Muted
Sovereign
The tree's
They whisper to me
I hear there pleas
To leave
There leaves fall
I echo
I echo
I echo the lost lonely call.

4. I Grow Tired

I grow tired of the same thing
Of doing a repetitive motion over and over again
Of living a life that is predictable
I grow tired of looking into
Up and down
Faces that show so much yet give nothing
I crave more and only know less
To give all I have
Is all I know
To give absolutely nothing is all I'm capable of
For this is all I know
I've experienced this before over and over
I've had people paraded in front of me
They stop
They talk
They stay sometimes longer then the last
Then they leave and I move on
And they
Move on
I grow tired of the same thing

My mind is sad and winding
Unwinding from its current knots
Falling and breaking and lost and lonely
I grow tired
I am restless
I grow tired of this

5. The Act of Rocking

Rocking forward then backwards
We move as one
We move like waves in the ocean
Choppy yet somehow at pace with another
We rock to a beat
Yet there is no sounds
We rock forwards then backwards
Then forwards again
You steady my rhythm and directed me back to calm
The rocking begins erratic
Anything to stop the sounds
Anything to stop the voices
We rock as one
You rock with me
And I struggle to breathe I feel your lips on my cheek
You kiss it
I feel the wetness
And the cool air hits
And I rock

Back and forth
Over and over untill the world starts to come to focus
We rock back and forth
We move like trees in the wind
Synchronized swimmers
Gold medalist at the art of rocking
We rock to bring the world back into focus
The act of rocking

The act of rocking
A sail
gently swaying in the breeze
The decision to fly a kite
On a windy day
The sway of the branches
as they lash against each other
The motion of a chair
On the front porch
Long forgotten
The feel of arms
Around you
As you cry
The comfort of a hand
In yours
As you walk
The act of rocking

6. Bathroom Floor

Time moves differently when your sitting on the floor in
the bathroom
It feels like it dosnt move at all
You see the light fade into darkness through the window
You see the dust piled in the corners
You think about how you should have cleaned this up a
long time ago
In the darkness you find yourself
Then you get lost in a thought
A thought that takes you to places
You don't want to go
Your twisting and falling
And forgetting what was to be forgotten
Your lost and
Alone
Thinking
And thinking
And thinking
Inside the bathroom

7. Nightmare

Nightmare
I remember you.
The way you talked.
The way you smelled.
The way you ...
Shhh it's a dream.
I wake up feeling your breath on my neck.
The stench of you all around.
... Shhh it's a dream .
I go to sleep picturing your faces
The evil glee in your eyes .
. . . Shhh it's a dream.
I study your faces in my mind wondering why you ...
.. . Shh its a dream .
I open my eyes and your not there
... Shhh it was Just adream.

8. Bird

Flying looks easy when your on the ground
Look at the birds
Dip and sway
The breeze pushes them
They glide in slow motion
Walking looks hard from the sky
Look at them
Jerk and trip
The ground slaps against there feet
They walk in slow motion
We are all going nowhere fast

9. The Edge of Nowhere

We are standing at the edge of a field
The sun is about to set in the sky
Tiny fluffs of cotton wood tree float
Around our heads
Birds fly above us
The grass flutters in the breeze
The stream behind us flows without a sound
This place feels like nowhere
Yet like somewhere important
Like this is where I should be
Next to you
I know when the sun sets
This will end
But for now
I'll stand beside you
At the edge of the field
In the place that feels
Like home

10. Shattered

Shattered
Beyond Smashed
Stepped on broken mangled trash
Compacted into the dirt
Always thrown away first
Fermenting Sulfa
From the mouth of a dead rat
Blood mixed with poison
Yes, that's what killed him
The curdled moldy cheese
Filled to the brim with wiggly things
He lay
Shattered
Beyond smashed
Compacted into the dirt
of course
Thrown away first
Fermented Sulfa
From the mouth of this dead rat
Blood mixed with poison

Yes,
That's surly what killed him

11. Quiet Strangulation

Quiet Strangulation
There is no air you can take in
No words that matter enough to be spoken
Breathe ragged but soft and broken
Candles flicker
In and out
Light there and gone
I wish the music would play
But I know its long gone
Nothing stays
Life feels like a blue tone maze
Follow the music
lead me to you
I'll love you on Sunday mornings
And on Mondays to
We can sleep in together and stay up until two
I can make you breakfast
Coffee for you and Tea for me
Quiet Strangulation
You took all my my air

Now i cant breathe

12. Oh Letter

Oh Letter,
How your words once consumed me
Consumed me whole
Like a grape
Grabbed me up
Chewed me into bits
Swallowed me whole
Oh letter,
How your words beacon to me
From across this room
I hear you speaking your words in my ear
Listen you say
Listen
Oh Letter,
How your words squeezed my heart
Like a hug
soft and warm
Bright and comfy
Delicious and Wholesome
Oh Letter,

How your words broke me
like a set of fine China
In the trash
smashed with a hammer
Thrown against the wall
Oh Letter,
Why do you exist
What was your purpose
But to hurt me
To warn me
To watch me
To break me
To make me completely yours
Oh Letter,
How your words own me
A leash around the neck of an obedient dog
yanking me away from the street
out of traffic
Yet I somehow wonder into a nearby hornets nest
As they sting my flesh over and over
I feel your words wrap around me
Crushing my windpipe
pulling me away from the bees
Back into your paper thin arms
Back to you
Oh Letter.

13. Star Bright Sky

Under star bright sky Next to swaying branches tussling
with thre neighbors
Hair dances in wind, preforming for the trees
Lips chapped and dry worried between teeth of white
Eyes burning and watering at the brims
Dirt and rocks under palms, course and rough
Feet shuffling forward and back through the grass
The moon glows casting shadows over a face
Sharp cool wind briskly shaves over shivering knee caps
and bare elbows
Thumbs tap a uneven beat on the ground
It plays along with the whooshing of the wind
A song
Hummed under breathe to break up the silence
Nose pink and chilled to the touch
Cheeks of rosy red inflamed with wind burn
Ears frozen to the sides of a head
Under star bright sky

14. Stagnant & Beside myself

Stagnate beside myself
Statuesque inside me
Stunningly oblique
It's true
I feel nothing
Not even for you
ha
You
Startling fake
BREAKE ME
Fucking stab me
Slither along behind me
Slink around looking for cause
Something to prove
Sounds like bad
Stupid is the feeling
Fuck feeling
Situated and silent
sleeping ?

no
Stuck?
maybe
Stagnant and beside myself
yes
safe is what i want
safe is all i need

15. Rainbow

The color orange
Always made me nauseous
Green leaf's give me peace
Yellow Sun bathes my skin in sweet kisses
Purple flowers remind me
Of what I've lost
Blue sky's make me hopeful
Brown Grass stabs me
With memories I don't want
Red sunsets wash over my eyes
In a wistful way

16. Filled

You Fill me in a way that
...Confuses me
In a way that steels the blood in my
Brain completely
Shaves off my ears and tarnishes my hearing
Chops off my arms and theirs is nothing left of me
Pressurizes the air
Inside my lungs
Until they pop and fall to the ground in smithereens
Flattens my throat like I'm a play thing
Stomps on my soul like this is a fate thing
And I cant stop the heating
You keep breaking
I keep Thinking
Why cant we just stop
stop and want the same thing

17. Glass eyes

Sad eyes
Oceans of Broken glass
The weather clears
Selfish sadness
Overwhelming grief
For a life untrue
Something that's not real
Clouds fade into the night
Mountains disapear
unwilling surrender
present but lost
to far gone to reach
Its useless
She's broken
see the glass
The glass that covers her skin
look
look at the glass in her eyes

18. So Quiet

It's so Quiet

The way a room can seem

It's so Quiet

I can't hear anything

It's so Quiet

I'm afraid to speak

It's so Quiet

To nervous to release the peace

It's so Quiet

My nerves they shake and sting

It's so Quiet

Just another broken thing

It's so Quiet

I don't want to feel like me

It's so Quiet

I've forgotten what its like to sing

It's so Quiet

I see the sway in the tree's

It's so Quiet

I just want to ...be

It's so Quiet
No sound, no one is listening
It's so Quiet
Down turned ears, cracked, shuddering
It's so Quiet
I wonder what its like to be byond hard of hearing
It's so Quiet
It's
So
Quiet

Sound,

Belittle me

19. The Same

I grow tired of the same thing
Of doing a repetitive motion over
And over...again
Of living a life that is predictable
I grow tired of looking into
Up and down
Faces that show so much yet give nothing
I crave more and only know less
To give all I know
Is all I know
To give absolutely nothing is all I'm capable of
For this is all I know
I've experienced this before over and over
I've had people parade in front of me
They stop
They talk
They stay sometimes longer then the last
Then they leave and I move on
And they
Move on

I grow tired of the same thing
My mind is sad and winding
Unwinding from its current knots
Falling and breaking and lost and lonely
I grow tired
I am restless
I grow tired of this

20. Silly

This is silly
This is never knowing
Confusing
The opposite of uplifting
Never content
I hate myself
And
Who I continue to be
I wish
I was anyone but me
Fuck you

No wait, Fuck me
Right?
Isn't that right
You make me want to cry
And sing at the same time
You make me like being me
I crave to be that free

21.

www.ingramcontent.com/pod-product-compliance
Lightning Source LLC
La Vergne TN
LVHW010834200726
843508LV00012B/2602